No Red Pen

Writers, Writing Groups & Critique

Victoria A. Hudson

What others are saying about *No Red Pen – Writers, Writing Groups & Critique*

"It's good to be reminded that "the basics" about how to be in or lead a writing group really do exist AND they can be clearly transmitted. In *No Red Pen,* a clear thinker and an incredibly organized writer takes us through all the steps. Every teacher of writing from high school through graduate school should have a copy of Vicki Hudson's very fine handbook. I found a gem in every chapter."
—Eloise Klein Healy, Founder and Editor, Arktoi Books, www.Arktoi.com, www.eloisekleinhealy@mac.com

"Allowing others to read and critique your work is not something a writer should take lightly. This smart book will help you avoid potential pitfalls and ensure that you understand the process. It is a valuable tool for writers!"
—Stephanie Chandler, author of several books including *The Author's Guide to Building an Online Platform*, www.StephanieChandler.com

"A good critique group should help you grow, not make you cower. Hudson has written a comprehensive guide to forming and maintaining a cower-free, supportive, honest, and enriching one. A must-read for anyone looking to start a fabulous writing group (or wanting to fix a broken one)!"
—Tanya Egan Gibson, author *How to Buy a Love of Reading*, www.tanyaegangibson.com

"Learning to give and to get a critique is an essential part of honing a writer's work. In this short, easy-to-digest book, Vicki Hudson offers invaluable, step-by-step advice on how critique partners can respectfully offer feedback so the writer actually can hear it and put it to use. This book should be required reading for every critique group!"
— Nina Amir, author of *How to Blog a Book,* www.copywrightcommunications.com

No Red Pen

Writers, Writing Groups & Critique

Victoria A. Hudson, M.F.A.

No Red Pen—Writers, Writing Groups, & Critique

By
Victoria A. Hudson

Copyright © 2012 by Victoria A. Hudson

Cover Photo Copyright © 2012 by Victoria A. Hudson

Cover Art by Joleen Naylor

Design by Patricia Rasch

Second Printing February 2012

Library of Congress Control Number: 2012902971

Gutterdog Press
P.O. Box 387
Hayward, CA 94543
http://vickihudson.com/

ISBN-13: 978-1470042134

ISBN-10: 1470042134

Manufactured in the United States

For my mother,
Susan Elizabeth Durfee Hudson

Still writing mom…

❧

Acknowledgements

First and always, my mother who never ceased encouraging me to tell stories and keep writing from when I started writing stories soon after I learned to read until I lost her, soon after my college graduation.

Those special teachers that took the time to help me grow as a writer just beginning and didn't let academia crush the writing spirit—Elizabeth Worthy (3rd grade), Alma Anthony and Rhoda Radow (Nova H.S.), and my University of Florida Freshman English teaching assistant, Vicki (Thompson?). The two professors from my MFA program at Saint Mary's College of California who most inspired and challenged me, Dr. Rosemary Graham and Professor Brenda Hillman.

Elizabeth Pomada, Michael Larsen and Laurie McLean who have created a community where writers of all levels thrive.

San Francisco Writers Conference Collegues Nina Amir and Amos White who have each contributed towards moving my writing forward.

Mary H. Webb for sharing wisdom of writing and life and so much more.

With appreciation for the encouragement and editorial expertise of Mary H. Webb and Tanya Egan Gibson. If any errors remain they are mine alone because I didn't pay attention.

Finally, my family who inspire and support me in all my endeavors and every day remind me what is really important.

Table of Contents

Introduction

No Red Pen—*Writers, Writing Groups & Critique* is intended for those writers looking for information on what to consider when forming or joining a writers' group and for writers seeking tools for critiquing work in progress. This is not a how-to book for writers' groups. There is no discussion of specific craft techniques. There are other books in the market that discuss finer points of writers' group administration and many that deal with craft. This book is intended to help the reader make informed choices in the marketplace of writing group workshops and provide useful skills for critique consumers. The act of entrusting one's written work and exposing that product of imagination, heart, and soul to the criticism of others is a risky and brave action by the writer and a privilege for the reader. *No Red Pen—Writers, Writing Groups & Critique* provides a toolbox for conducting a writers' workshop and recommendations for critique that fundamentally respects the writer and the work.

This small book was initially a germ of an idea from many conversations with friend and mentor Mary H. Webb while I was a member of her community college fiction writing class in Berkeley, California. There I was introduced to her Three Stage Method for writing workshops Later, when I entered an MFA program, my appreciation for this method grew even stronger, as the workshop formula used in the MFA program seemed to me at times to distract from the writing process, ignore healthy boundaries between the participants, and fail to fundamentally respect the writing and the writer. One instructor allowed only positive criticism, shutting down any comment the instructor perceived as negative, a stricture that fundamentally stifled growth. MFA candidates at other institutions have told me about having similar experiences to mine when their workshops followed traditional techniques. Many described their experience as brutal and cutthroat, far worse than what I experienced at my institution. I knew from my time with Mary H. Webb that a workshop did not need to be that way. I knew that the work and the writer could be given specific and difficult critique in a respectful environment that would encourage rather than discourage continued writing as well as provide positive, affirming feedback. I encouraged her to publish her method. She encouraged me to share what I had learned.

I've also been a member of different community based writer groups over the years and found that the drama and personal dynamics of varying individuals often distracted from the group critiquing honestly and effectively. Sometimes we just didn't really know what we were doing despite our good intentions. Sometimes individual agendas got in the way. I have taken part in physical groups that meet in a brick and mortar location and in virtual online communities. Both venues have value, and both have disadvantages. When choosing a group, the writer must know what is needed at the time and what her own limitations and threshold for participation as a group member are in order to make an informed decision when selecting what type of group to join.

I was honored in 2009 when Elizabeth Pomada and Michael Larsen, Co-founders and Co-directors of the San Francisco Writers Conference (SFWC), invited me to participate on a 2010 SFWC panel about critique groups and invited me back in 2011 and 2012. One of the handouts I created for those workshops was revised and developed and then sent out into the wild, finding acceptance for publication by The Writer, as an article "How to Give Good Feedback" in the May 2011 print issue and on its website.

What I learned from Mary Webb and her Three Stage Method, and from my experience as a participant in differing types of writing groups has given me insight into what works and what, (at least for me and many of my peers) does not work as well. Bringing a piece of writing into a workshop is not license for other people to subject you to a brutal, critical process as a rite of passage. Workshopping a piece does not need to be a hazing ritual.

There are many ways to give feedback, and many ways to run a workshop or writers group. Fundamentally, the choice comes down to what the individual choosing to join such a formal or informal group (program, workshop, or seminar) hopes to achieve in the process while ensuring that the process does not negate the effort of the work. The agreement between writer and critique provider (be that instructor or peer,) should include mutual respect for the work, the process, and the participants. A process that is destructive and hostile, that discourages rather than encourages is not a method that weeds out weak writers, just one that stifles those that often have had their voices muzzled in other ways as well.

Everyone has a story. No one else can tell your story. The process of creating, refining and ultimately releasing it into the wild that is publication in the world needs to be a respectful one. *No Red Pen—Writers, Writing Groups & Critique* is not an overview of writing groups—it is a manifesto for a different paradigm for workshopping and critiquing. *No Red Pen—Writers, Writing Groups & Critique* is a product of what I have learned along my journey and if it aids another emerging writing along the way, cool beans.

Why Critique Groups?

Why do writers join critique groups?

Writers join critique groups for a variety of reasons. The fundamental purpose in joining a critique group is to receive feedback on your work. The intention is to improve and become a better writer. A critique group can provide its members with far more than just feedback. The critique group provides the writer a family sized community of people fundamentally there for a common goal. This is the writer's support group. These are the people that follow and support her development. This is the cheering section that aids the writer onwards toward her goals. These are the trusted companions that journey together towards publishing and getting the work out in the world. The group is the writer's immediate network of colleagues that conduct the word-of-mouth marketing campaign when the work is in the world. These are the first members of the writer's social network that click on the "like" button, follow her in the social media world, and help her get exposure by including the writer's postings on their virtual presence in that environment. A writer's critique group is the writer's team.

Why do writers quit critique groups?

Because they are not having their needs met. Like any team, family, or group, there are interpersonal dynamics. A writer can feel like no one "gets" her writing. A writer who experiences the feedback process as hostile will tire of feeling trashed and leaving the meetings with hurt feelings. The group may not be challenging enough. The group may give genuinely nice feedback, but if the writer feels that really tough issues are never addressed and that the work is not improving, the group time is not a productive investment. The group is just a bunch of individuals, and sometimes there are too many competing goals and expectations.

Why do writers not seek out a critique group?

Fear. The writer critique group is an acknowledgement that the writer seeks more than just putting words on the page. Joining and participating in a critique group is a huge act of faith that exposes individual vulnerability. No one likes to feel vulnerable and unsure. We have survival instincts that temper involvement in the unknown and risk taking when a possible outcome could be painful—physically, emotionally, or mentally. Some writers cannot make that leap of trust to join a critique group because they fear the unknown or anticipate discomfort at sharing the very personal product that is a writer's work.

Here is the bottom line: The work not being "liked" is not important. What *is* important is why a reader might not like the work. Answer the question "Why don't you like the work?" This gives the writer information. And information is what the writer needs to become a better writer.

Learn to give useful, effective information. Learn how to create a group that ensures respectful dialogue between readers and writers, in which members give each other useful, effective information. Then you will have a critique group that challenges, supports, and enables the writer's journey to authorship. Learn how to deliver feedback so you may deliver the strongest criticism in a manner that ensures the writer walks away still feeling good about the writing and wants to continue on the journey. Have tools in your own toolbox that make you an effective member of a group, know what is needed to build an effective group from the start or to reassess a current group to improve its functioning, or be able to recognize when a group is more dysfunctional than productive.

What if they don't like it?

A good critique, even when it includes what could be perceived as negative criticism is not about if the reader "liked" it. A skillfully provided critique does not need to say, "I didn't like your story/poem/essay." (Not to say that hearing someone likes your work isn't nice to hear, because it is nice to hear, and there is a place for that in the conversation between critique reader and writer.) What a skillfully provided critique will include is some variation on "My response when I read your work was (fill in the blank). What didn't work is…" Or, "This is what caused my reaction of…" The skilled critique provider does not make the feedback personal even when including personal details of response. The skilled provider is able to see internally what is beneath the experienced response or emotion and explain in specific terms and language the experience or impact of the work. This gives the writer information that is useful.

Far more useful than:
"I didn't like it."
"I liked it."

Remember—

- A critique group is the writer's team.

- Writers leave when their needs aren't met, the experience is hostile, not challenging enough, or unproductive.

- Fear keeps the writer from seeking critique.

- Respectful dialogue mitigates fear.

- Why someone doesn't like the work is important, liking or not liking is only interesting.

Where To Find A Group

In this age of information, there are countless ways to locate a writers' group.

Formal groups are often academic in nature, part of a program of study such as the Master of Fine Arts degree or an undergraduate creative writing course. There are hundreds of writing workshop programs that meet over a finite period of time with an established author. Many of such workshops or seminars are very well known and long running. Formal programs usually have an application process that requires a sample of your writing and a recommendation or reference from someone familiar with your work. Formal programs usually have a cost associated with participation. Often there is financial aid available upon application. Both the entry process and the financial aid process are competitive. Writing classes in person or via distributed or distance (online) learning are all viable avenues for writing development. These types of groups usually have a well established structure.

Informal groups are usually community based regardless of how community is defined. The group may meet in real time at a physical location or asymmetrically in a virtual or web based location. Members are recruited by word of mouth, advertisements in community or weekly papers, flyers at bookstores or coffee shops, or online via web page, Facebook or Twitter. There is usually little or no financial investment required of the writer who joins one of these groups. Established and successful groups may meet over years with little turnover of members. Entry when new members are recruited may have a semi-competitive element or the group may simply use an interview process or trial attendance period.

Writing conferences provide a wealth of networking potential and the possibility of meeting and connecting with other like minded writers who may know about or start a group you can connect with. Two resources for information on writing programs and writing events for formal writing workshops and seminars are The Association of Writers and Writing Programs (AWP) and Poets & Writers. Two particularly useful online writing communities include Writing.com and Ladieswhocritique.com. There are many, many other genre and non-genre specific options online that include discussion and descriptions of writing resources for the developing writer. If a writer wants to join a group, the only challenge may be in finding the right one.

Remember—

- Two types of groups: Formal, often academic or seminar based with an application process and often financial investment required, and informal community based.

- Writing conferences, online resources, community papers, community bulletin boards are all places to find out about critique groups.

- Entry can be competitive.

- Some groups are long standing with little turnover or are designed for short cycles of work.

Groups can be virtual/online or in person.

Fear

Fear is a huge reason why people don't join a writers' group or seek out criticism, yet we know that feedback is essential to the writing process. Fear keeps writers from ever moving a manuscript from the drawer to the mailbox. Fear gets in the way. A writer venturing into the world of critique groups or returning after a poor group experience has a valid emotion when experiencing fear. Let's not belittle the power of fear.

Fear, however, can also be a friend. Fear is a little voice that taps you on the shoulder and says, "Psst, pay attention." Fear in a critique group is fear of failure; fear no one will like the writer, the work will be rejected, the people will be mean, the feedback will hurt, the process will be too difficult... There are many, many reasons to fear the unknown in venturing into a group of people, usually strangers (at least in the beginning) to whom the writer will expose her product of imagination or experience and hard work. One of the biggest fears an emerging or new writer has is that no one will like the work that has been labored over and poured out with heartfelt dedication.

"This is my heart and soul," the writer says, "Do you like it?" Meaning of course, do you like *me*?

For a writer that wants to improve, the first step is letting go of that fear. Recognize that the writing is not the writer's identity. The writing is not the writer's self. The writing is just words on a page that create an experience for the reader to share and immerse oneself within. The writing (even when you are telling a story where you are the main character) is not about you, the writer.

Letting go, in any aspect of life, is just plain difficult. It is not like we have a little button to click in the brain, the Letting Go Button. Letting go is a huge psychological process. Like any skill developed over time, with practice, the skill of letting go becomes if not easier, then more streamlined, faster, unconscious in its effort.

Successful letting go requires acknowledgement that there is something to let go of. In terms of joining a critique group, the writer must make the movement from not being in a group to joining and participating in a group. When fear is the obstacle in the way of the movement, and that fear is not acknowledged, all manner of other reasons will manifest: No time, don't know how, don't know where to find one, don't know what to do in one, the work isn't ready… If you really want to join a group, none of these issues is a true obstacle. Let's face it, "The work isn't ready." That is the whole point of the group, to help get the work ready! So, let's go back to fear and letting it go.

Acknowledge that fear is the problem in the way. If you can focus specifically on what you are afraid of, that may be helpful though it's not all that necessary at this stage. Notice how attached you are to that nice, comfortable fear? It's what you know, it's what you've been with for a while. Really, isn't that fear a little like a buddy you've had with you a long time, sort of your teddy bear for not doing things? Think about letting that fear go be on its own now without you. Oh, there, did you feel that—that little twinge of guilt? That reflex of loyalty to what you've always known?

Fear is comfortable. Fear can be cozy. Fear can be a good friend or a frenemy. You get to choose. Once you are aware of your fear, you get to choose what to do with the fear. Let it lead the way, or let it move to the background and while present, fear is not in control. Sometimes we take our teddy bears with us long after we have outgrown them just because it makes venturing out into the unknown easier. Eventually, when we are ready, we put the teddy bear away, on its shelf. You can do the same thing with that fear that gets in the way of joining a critique group.

"I'm afraid to join a writers' group." Good acknowledgement.

"I can be afraid and still join a writers' group." Now you

have moved forward and started to let go.

What does fear the friend whisper to you as you move forward?

"Pssst. Be safe. Take care of you."

What is the worst that could happen?

Complete strangers who have no obligation to say nice things, won't.

Mere acquaintances, who don't know or care about little me, will slice and dice my heartfelt story.

These strangers, the competition, the perceived experts will tear me apart.

Oh wait, not me, the work.

So what enables a writer to put her work out there for critique?

Simply, have good boundaries. Like just about every other situation in life, good boundaries in a writing group keep us safe, promote civility and provide guidance for interaction. This is the work and this is the person who wrote the work. The feedback is about the work, not about the person. Not liking the work is not equal to not liking the person.

Boundaries make it safe for fear to not lead the way. A good sense of boundaries in terms of your writing means an understanding of where you, the individual is, and where the writing begins. The individual has many facets and aspects of identity. The writing is a product of the individual's work, imagination and skill but is not the *whole* of the writer. Writers have a relationship with their writing and like other personal relationships, the lines can become blurred. Recognize that you, the writer, are *not* the product, the writing. Separate yourself from what is produced and it will be easier to hear criticism. You will not take the critique personally because you understand the critique is not about you.

Demonstrating a healthy relationship with your writing encourages healthy interaction with those who would offer critique. Have a sense of self that is greater than the writing. Now when you invite critique, you are not inviting criticism of self, merely feedback on the work. Your critique readers will appreciate that as it invites honest feedback that isn't limited by concern for the writer's feelings.

Freedom to give honest feed back is not license for abuse, disrespect or insult.

Remember—

- Feedback is important, yet fear can get in the way.
- Fear is powerful, yet fear is also good as it helps with awareness and self-care.
- The work is not the writer's identity, not liking the work and not liking the writer are not the same.
- Letting go of fear is hard and takes practice.
- Acknowledge the fear is the first part of letting go.
- Fear can be comfortable.
- Fear just wants you to pay attention.
- Good boundaries mitigate fear.
- Critique is not about you, it is about the writing.
- Have a healthy relationship with your writing encourages healthy interactions with the critiquer.
- Freedom for honest feedback is not license for abuse, disrespect, or insult.

The Critique Provider

Critique comes in several flavors. Critique as part of a group. Critique written on the page. Critique verbally. Critique done by the writer as part of the revision process. Fundamental to any critique is respect for the work. Respect for the work needs to guide all aspects of critique. If you have respect for the work, it will not matter how you feel personally about the writer. If you respect the work, you will have healthy boundaries as you critique the work and not let any personal issues that may exist with the writer migrate into the feedback about the work.

"But the writer wants me to like him."

Maybe so, but that isn't why the writer joined the group. If the writer just wanted to be part of a group for social interaction, there are far easier and less taxing groups one can join. The writer wants to become a better writer.

When you take part in a critique group, you give and accept an implied promise: We will honestly evaluate the writing offered. We will provide honest feedback. What is often missing from groups or workshops is the third pillar of the agreement: We will treat the work and the writer with respect regardless of the depth or type of criticism offered. A three-legged table won't provide much stability. Here is the fourth leg of the agreement: The writer is part of the process.

Remember—

- Foundation for any type of critique is respect for the work.

- Respect prevents personal issues from infecting the critique.

- Writers join critique groups fundamentally to become better writers.

- The promise: Honestly evaluate the writing, provide honest feedback, treat the work and writer with respect, and remember the writer is part of the process.

The Group

There are many types of groups or workshops for writing critique. Before getting to the method to use in the group, first determine what kind of group you want to be involved with.

Yes, back to boundaries also known as rules. If rules is too harsh a term, think of them as guidelines or agreements for how to function. Anarchy has its place in human endeavors, but if you want to have an effective group with reduced potential for drama and mayhem, consider a few guidelines.

Considerations when going into or forming a group:

- What size group
- How often will each writer have work read/ critiqued
- Submission length

- Frequency of meeting
- Location of meeting
- Genre specific or mixed genre
- Expectations
- Goals
- Gender, culture, ethnicity
- Physical vs virtual
- Craft
- Critique guidelines

There are likely many other considerations that would be important to consider. If they are not covered in this list just add them to your own list of concerns.

What size group?

The group needs to be a manageable size so all members receive an equable opportunity to receive feedback. The giving of critique is the tradeoff for receiving critique so how often the writer will be on the receiving end is a fair concern. This is partially impacted by the process decisions: will every writer submit and read every week or will there be a rotation process? More specifically, the size of the group impacts how much time the group has. Think of time as a resource that fuels the function of the group. How much time do the group members have between group meetings to devote to the work of creating the critique? How much time is available for the meetings? How much time is there in each meeting for each group member to read or give feedback? Parse it out to help determine how large or small the group should become based upon the varying time demands.

How often will each writer's work be submitted to the group for critique?

In one model, everyone contributes a piece to be worked each meeting. The upside of this is writers have a stricter deadline for work to be brought in; the down side is the time available in the group for the actual process of delivering feedback is rationed more significantly. A second method uses a rotation process. Not all writers submit work for critique each meeting. The advantage of this is a greater amount of time for dividing both in terms of deadlines and for receipt of the feedback in the group meeting. Using the rotation model, there is more time to spend on a each work considered.

Deciding who submits when is as simple as a signup done at the beginning of a workshop cycle. The cycle spreads over a predetermined number of meetings. Upon conclusion, a new signup is generated. The rotation can also be determined by genre, alphabetical order, seniority or lack of seniority in the group, or random drawing of lots. Really, whatever method the group determines works for it. The key here is that the group decides on and agrees to a method for determining who will put forward work and when.

Time is an important resource regardless of the method used. For example, a ten person group that meets for three hours once a week, allowing for 15 minutes of administrative time on either end of the meeting, must divide 150 minutes between ten writers when all submit work at each meeting. That is 15 minutes of group feedback for each piece. That works out to just about a minute and half of feedback per each of those nine people per piece. The numbers are not important, the formula is. Total number of minutes minus admin time, divided by number of writers submitting each meeting equals number of minutes available for each writer's work to be critiqued in the group meeting. Look at that as N(umber of total minutes minus admin time) $\div$ W(riters) submitting each meeting = A(vailable) minutes for each writer's work during the meeting. $(N \div W = A)$ Now, A(vailable) number of minutes for each work divided by R(eaders) equals I(ndividual) allotment of total minutes each reader has to deliver the critique. $(A \div R = I)$ If the writer gets an opportunity to talk too, then R is constant to how many participants are in the group. When the number of submitters is smaller, the number of minutes allotted per piece goes up.

Two formulas very useful: $N \div W = A$ and $A \div R = I$. If you consider length of time to actually read the piece, the numbers change again. Total available time (N) must be reduced to allow for reading.

Apologies to math geeks, the author was an English major.

What is the equable division of time for members of the group to receive fair and considered critique? Submitting once a month, every week, or once a quarter? What does the writer need, and what workload can the group sustain? Figure that one out and you have the answer for what is an equable division of time.

Length of submission

This may not seem like a very crucial decision to make yet logistically, the length of the submission is a linchpin in the fairness foundation of the group. Everyone is busy. Everyone has lives and family and work obligations as well as maybe pets and hobbies and other organizations that meet and demand time. Time is a resource, and parsing out how much time is needed from a member both in the group and preparing for the group is important. Remember the implied promise is to honestly evaluate the writing offered. That requires some measure of investment of personal time so that the feedback offered is reasoned, considered, and not without thought. The work submitted must be read more than once and then carefully considered. Approach the work as you would want your work approached. In order to support that throughout the group, respect that everyone has a limited resource called time to give to the group in between meetings. How many pages can the group members be reasonably expected to read between meetings and provide useful, in depth feedback? The number of pages in a submission is impacted by how often and how many people submit each workshop cycle. Consider if five writers have work critiqued each group meeting and each writer submits twenty pages the week before their work is covered in the group meeting. That is one hundred pages of reading a week. If it takes you a minute to read a page normally plus several minutes to read critically, plus ten minutes to write a minimal critique—that is 90 minutes per piece. Or 7.5 hours each week to prepare critique for five members of the group. Do the math to figure out the logistics. Be reasonable—not too small a sample, not too large.

Frequency of meeting

Weekly, monthly, quarterly—there are a number of factors at play with frequency of meeting. For the most part, a beginning writers' group will benefit from a more structured frequency of meetings, once a week or twice a month for example. Frequency should be determined by what the writers want or need and where they are in the writing process. Are you critiquing initial works? More frequent meetings would probably be a benefit. Are you critiquing finished drafts of complete works now in revision? Longer periods between meetings that support reading and working with larger pieces may be needed. If the purpose of the group is partly to provide the writer with a consistent structure that will both support and guide the writing, then frequent meetings are a good choice. Try once a week or every other week. Become acquainted with the demands of a writing group, of being part of a team of people that you depend upon and that depends upon you with the common goal of improved writing. What works for you? What enables you to devote the required time so that when you critique you provide reasoned, well considered feedback? Know what you can do and what your available resources are and determine the frequency based upon that.

Location of meeting

Will you meet at someone's house? Will you meet at a local office space, someone's workplace, in a rented space (How will you fund that?) Will location rotate among members? Will you use a public space—a restaurant, bar, pub, coffee shop, a park? The environment of the meeting space influences the productivity of the meeting. If the meeting takes place in a public space, do you have adequate privacy to discuss writing that involves deeply personal issues? Is the noise level a distraction? Do people outside of the group recognize this meeting is closed to outside observers? Does every member need to purchase something in order to legitimize use of the public space? Is the physical environment too cold, too hot, or subject to the seasons? In a private space are there distracters such as dogs, spouses, kids? In someone's home, is there an issue of allergens (pet hair, cats, smoking)?

Consider that your writers' group is a form of workplace. The intent is be productive and improve a work product—the writing. Approach the location with the same intention you would have if creating a work related meeting. Find a place that is productive and supportive to the objectives of the meeting. Not to say you can't have fun at your meetings, but have fun that supports the objectives.

Genre specific or mixed genre

Will the group concentrate on one genre or be a mixed genre group? There are advantages to either choice. A beginning group that is learning how to function as a group and learning critique skills may be better off with one genre in the group. Then all members have a common point of reference for what is being written. Science fiction writers, for example, will have the common ground of having read many of the same authors and will understand the commonly accepted parameters of the genre (the three laws of robotics for example) that someone unfamiliar with the genre may not understand. A group of poets will understand and speak the language of poetry's mechanics that might sound foreign to a novelist. Shared perspective creates a common basis for understanding, which in itself creates a starting point.

Experienced critique group members may find a benefit in the differing perspectives that people writing in different genres may bring to their work. A poet may give a nonfiction writer an outstanding critique on imagery for example. The fiction writer may be able to effectively assist a nonfiction writer struggling with scene versus summary.

A disadvantage of a genre specific group is that a group can become too insular about that specific type of writing. A disadvantage of a non-genre specific group is that the group could be too disparate with the members all speaking different "languages" and not having their needs met because their group-mates are unfamiliar with the conventions of their genres.

Expectations and goals

Going into the group, the writer must have some level of self awareness about the group's intended purpose (goal) and its anticipated outcome (expectation). Does the writer just want people to read the work? If so, a readers' group where writers just come and read may be more appropriate. Does the writer want a social group? If so, look elsewhere or look for a social writing group. A social writing group is more about fellowship than the process of improving the writing. The writing is really just a reason to justify getting together because for some reason, members can't just say,

"Hey, I want to hang out with writers, talk writing, tell stories, maybe share work all just for fun with no actual goal." That is a social writers' group, where critique is not the main function. Does the writer want feedback with the intent to improve and better the piece and the writer's craft? That person will make a good critique group member.

When interviewing for a group, remember the interview is a two way process. The group interviews prospective members; the potential member interviews the group. Clarify the expectations. What does the group expect from its members? What does the writer want from the group? Does the writer expect assistance with achieving writing goals such as getting a piece published, completing a novel or poetry collection, or attaining an agent? Does the writer want support with marketing, and platform building? Is there an assumption that if a member of the group reads publically, the group will show up? Will the group Facebook, Twitter, and blog about members who are attaining publishing and authorship goals? Or, are members there just for the critique, leaving the rest to other facets of the writers' lives? Does the group expect certain agreements (established expectations) from its members?

Group agreements establish a fair playing field for everyone participating. These are the group boundaries—things like number of pages submitted, standards for format, and participation expectations. Honoring boundaries creates a respectful environment. Establishing group expectations ensures that everyone knows what the boundaries are. It is important to identify the parameters the group (team) will operate within. For example, if the group does not establish page limits for submissions, then the reading process becomes unsustainable. Some might submit ten pages; others thirty pages. Do the math—if five writers submit at the weekly meeting and they all submit twenty pages, that is one hundred pages each each week. Time is the resource that fuels the process, and if writers abuse that reserve, then the quality of the critique is reduced. If there are no limits, then eventually the writers who make an effort to submit pieces that are workable in limited time frames will be resentful of those that submit mega-pieces and expect the same level of in depth critique. Consider the sustainability of this week after week.

Expectations for format: This should be a no brainer, yet there are always those that push the limit. Really, use double spaced lines on pages with one inch margins all around. That is the professional standard for submission. Why do any different with your critique group?

Participation: If you submit work to be read, then you must read and critique work by others too. There are no free rides in a critique group. Members are on an expedition together. The price for passage is time invested in providing fair and honest critiques. In return, the writer journeys towards improvement by receiving critiques from the rest of the group.

Process: The group has an established means for conducting its process. Members agree to follow the process. What happens when members fail to follow the agreements? What is the process for leaving the group or being left by the group? Reduce drama with clear communicated expectations.

Bottom line: What parameters does the group need its members to agree to that will ensure a respectful, productive, effective group? Define them. Communicate them to everyone. Get everyone's agreement. Whether you decide on them as a group or have them decided upon by the individual who starts a group, in the end, the group must decide to adopt and accept them. As an individual interviewing for the group, find out what those expectations are before committing yourself. If the group can't identify a key process and its foundation of operation, its agreements, then it might not be the group that will give you the best experience. Look elsewhere, or start up a group if needed.

Gender, culture, ethnicity

Are the members of the group all the same gender? A women's writing group or a men's writing group? What about the transgender writer? Do you want a mixed group? Do men critique differently from women, straight men from gay men? One type of group may create a safer environment for some writers, while for other writers this group fails to provide much needed feedback due to its homogeneity. A writer may need a more restricted membership at one stage of the work than a later one. The writer must determine what components in terms of gender, culture or ethnicity will help or hinder her development and choose a writing group accordingly. The selection is not in stone. As the writing develops, the writer's skill at craft and critique develops, and her level of security and safety in terms of being part of a group develops. Seek out or create what you need when you need it. Be honest with yourself about the type of readers from whom you can't really hear feedback from right now regardless of how skillfully it is provided. For instance, if you're writing a memoir about child sexual abuse, maybe having a person the gender of that abuser in your group will hinder your process. Maybe not. If you're writing a novel based upon the south Miami drag queen camp culture, maybe having to explain the cultural references to straight males would hinder your process. On the other hand, maybe it would give you insight into where your writing needs improvement in order to be marketable to a larger segment of the reading population.

You're writing a collection of poetry that speaks to the immigrant experience of a minority faith group in the United States. You're writing a collection of essays about women's combat experience in the middle east. You're writing short stories focused upon foster care.

You're writing... You can be writing about anything. Some members of a mixed group may not "get" the experience. At different stages of your process, it may not feel safe to be in a group with others that don't reflect at least in some way your own experience. If that is true, then pick a group that mirrors what you need so you can be a fully functioning part of the group. When you are ready, move on to wider, more inclusive groups because everyone has a perspective that could be useful in critique.

Physical verses virtual

With the ease of the internet, there are far more venues for writing groups now than in the days before virtual existence. Physical groups have their own advantages: being in the same room itself lends towards civility. Perhaps one could argue you have a better chance of getting to know each other. Those that have deep relationships with online friends may argue about that. Going to the meeting gets you out of the house—a very attractive enticement to the stay-at-home mom who wrangles a toddler every day. (Adult conversation, WOOHOO!) Human contact and interaction have value. Looking the writer in the eye, and seeing the body language as the work is read or critiqued provides information to the writer. A disadvantage is that the group meetings have to be physically accessible to all members of the meeting within reasonable commute distance from home or work and be in an environment conducive to the work. The internet can support the physical group. E-mail can be used to distribute work to be critiqued before the meeting or to maintain communication between meetings. The group can create a website that highlights the work of the group members, post the schedule of events, or readings, and announce calls for new members.

A virtual group, be that in a simulated environment where avatars interact in a virtual space or over the web of the internet does not require that everyone is within a reasonable distance. Cyber writing groups may have members from anywhere in the world. Juggling time zones for meetings might become an issue, but then again the whole concept of the "meeting" comes into question. Use a discussion board to post work and critiques. Schedules can be posted for the review periods, when to post critique, and when the writer interacts with the critique.

Numerous writing oriented online communities exist where work can be posted and feedback received. The community itself will usually have its own guidelines for how to interact and what is expected from its participants. This can open your work to a large population of potential reviewers. Be conscious that just as in small groups, not everyone will be skilled at critiquing. Assess for yourself what the value of these groups is to you. Within these communities, there may also be means for establishing smaller, more selective groups. Certainly, this is something worth exploring if online is the way you want to go.

Craft

What are the expectations regarding craft and craft development in the group? Will the group concentrate solely on reading work and providing critique, or will the group also provide for development of craft? Will some meetings include development work: Writing prompts, discussion of craft, or study of examples of craft; or will created work and its critique be the sole focus? What is the writer's expectation: Do you want a group that helps develop craft with a more hands on, experiential method (prompts, study) or develops craft via receipt and application of what is learned from the critique of your work? Join the group that meets your craft expectations.

Critique guidelines

How do you critique as a member of a group verbally and on the page, or when doing a self critique for revision?. Fundamentally, this is where civility and respect must be paramount. Honest feedback must occur that is fairly considered and rendered with respect. When done right, then even the hardest information the writer might hear is delivered in a manner that is not threatening. The writer must feel good about writing, about continuing the endeavor even after hearing that the work that has been labored over so long and hard has significant issues that prevent it from being an effective piece of writing.

There are many ways to accomplish critique, many ways to workshop writing. Is there a right way or a wrong way? Fundamentally, if the process of critique causes the writer to no longer want to write, that method is not a healthy procedure for it fails to respect the writing and the process that brought the writing into existence.

Remember—

- What kind of group do you want? What considerations are important to you?

- What are the boundaries, agreements and expectations?

- A group that can't articulate its agreements and expectations is ripe for mayhem and misunderstanding. Group agreements establish a fair playing field.

- What is the group's intended goal?

- Interviewing for a group is a two way process.

- If the process causes the writer to no longer want to write, that method is not a healthy procedure.

- $N \div W = A$ and $A \div R = I$. If you consider length of time to actually read the piece, the numbers change again. Total available time (N) must be reduced to allow for reading.

Critique

Group Process

After numerous writers' groups, writer retreat workshops, academic writing programs (to include the MFA) the best method this author has experienced is Author and Playwright Mary H. Webb's Three Stage Method. "The Three Stage Method is designed to protect you as a writer and as a human being while giving you the very best constructive criticism that other writers can provide. Human beings tend to cling to the negative statements made about their work when that work is very close to their heart, mind, or soul. And what other kind of work is worth the amount of time and effort invested in writing?" (Webb)

The Three Stage Method takes time to learn well. It takes practice. But once mastered, it is an exceptionally flexible tool and a virtual guarantee that in discussions about people's writing no one will sustain permanent psychic damage, be emotionally scarred, or give up the writing life because the critique experience is damaging or the individual fails to thrive as a writer. The Three Stage Method when utilized in a group ensures that both readers and the writer, have a voice. Information is gathered, communicated, and supported.

The following description of the Three Stage Method is based in part upon Webb's handouts and assumes the reader reads her work in the group. This method works equally well if the reading occurs outside of the group meeting. Reading in the group is the preferred method.

Being able to listen to the language while the work is read aloud with the intended emphasis and intonation that the writer gives her work is very useful. If you are hearing a work for the first time, make notes when words, phrases, or lines catch your attention so you can read them back to the writer later. Take notice of your emotional responses and jot them down with reference to where they occurred or specific lines that take hold of you. When something takes you out of the immersion of the journey, take note so you can mention that to the writer later.

STAGE ONE—After the writer reads her work, the rest of the group makes positive statements about it ONLY. If you have no positive statements to make about the piece of writing, remain quiet. But if you learn to listen really actively, to try and imagine what the writer concerned was trying to say, you may find that your mind will open up and you will appreciate new ways of writing, new insights. Language should also be discussed during Stage One. When a writer hears another person repeat sentences, written images or lines that the reader liked particularly, those sentences or lines become deeply implanted in the writer's mind. This leads to the development of a distinctive voice and style of one's own. The critique providers are speaking to the writer, not about the writer or the writing as an inanimate object. Speaking to the person rather than with the writer as a fly-on-the-wall observer invites a degree of civility that is often missing when the writer is not part of the process.

STAGE TWO—The writer has an opportunity to seek specific information. The writer now asks questions of the rest of the group. This stage is essential for effective criticism. You MUST be responsible as a writer when you submit work for consideration and critique and prepare your own questions in advance to ask the workshop or critique group. If you fail to do so, do not be surprised when you get very little effective constructive criticism. This is where the writer can channel some of the critique towards what matters to her most. You may ask anything—about the end of the story, language, plot, sequencing, rough transitions, or whatever aspect of the work you have produced you may be struggling with, feel unsure about, or about which you just want specific input. The important thing is to have at least one or two questions prepared in advance because the process of critique is a partnership between the writer and the critique providers.

STAGE THREE—This stage is also indispensable for effective and constructive criticism. During this final stage of the group process, members in the group make UNSOLICITED constructive critical suggestions. In other words, they are not responding to the writer's questions. These are the comments that come directly from the reader's experience and are unrelated in any shape or form to the writer's experience. These comments MUST be made carefully. The interests of the writer submitting the work for consideration are still being protected. Stage Three does not give a blanket permission to be vicious and nasty.

If you are saying things in a way that you would not like them said to you, then you are definitely failing to provide critique in a respectful manner. Civility, respect for the writer and the writing is paramount here. So learn to phrase things carefully with respect for other writers. But do not skip this stage just because it takes time to learn to do it well. Do not forego this stage because it is difficult or demanding in terms of your skills as a member of a group. Concerns you might want to raise will include: plot, rough transitions, dialogue, the balance of scene and summary, falling out of point of view, superfluous characters, faulty sequencing or pacing, to list only a few. Discussion of technique is appropriate in Stage Three. Anything that relates to craft is useful in Stage Three. Anything that caused a response in you that created a sense of "didn't like" is what you need to dissect so you can get at the issue beneath the surface rejection. This is the important information for the writer. Not that you didn't like the work. Rather, why did you dislike the work? What made you uncomfortable? What made you angry?

In Stage Three the potentially negative information is communicated. It may be that your response is "personal" in a way that has nothing to do with the craft and is thus irrelevant to the writing. What is relevant is that you had an emotional response. If this is so, than Stage Three will also allow the writer to understand this. If you communicate in a respectful manner, then the negative connotation of criticism is removed. What you communicate is just information for the writer to consider in order to improve the piece. The information is not an attack on the writer or a devaluing of the work.

The language you choose when giving a critique is important. Words such as cliché, trite, hackneyed, politically correct, politically incorrect, isms or stereotypes are labels that are defined differently by different people. When used, they may do incalculable damage to other people. They are shortcuts that fail to define why a word, phrase, or characterization creates an obstacle in the writing. These words are common in our culture, yet have different meanings to different people based upon their different experiences. They are shortcuts that fail to provide any real information for the writer precisely because they have different meanings for different people. They are code for discomfort or anger or a diverse experience of response.

What do you really mean? Instead of using code words, define what you are trying to express, what is beneath the easy label you are applying. Do that, and you provide useful information. Do the hard work of defining that emotional response in you, the reader, so the writer has accurate, specific feedback.

Don't ask someone if what they read/wrote "really happened." It is irrelevant and none of your business. If the author wishes to "confess" that the work is autobiographical, that is her prerogative. The reality of the experience created on the page is not pertinent or needed in order for a reader to create an effective review or critique of the work. So don't waste your own and the group's precious time with an irrelevant and rude comment such as, "Is this true?"

In short, being an artist does not give you license to be petty, eaten up by jealousy or vicious. Being writers, we have room to express ourselves which is an extravagance. Use it with intention. If you take the time to learn and apply the Webb Three Stage Method, the process will reward you well with effective criticism conducted in a respectful manner that encourages continued writing while improving craft and the eventual product, *the writing,* the work produces.

Individual Process

Perhaps you are not in a formal writing group but have one of more writing friends who ask you to occasionally read and comment on their work. Or maybe you want greater skill in self-critique so when you revise your own work, you are more productive and effective with your own revisions. The same skills apply, and you can follow a similar process when giving an individual critique as when part of a group. Adapt the group process to the individual effort.

Remember—

- The Webb Three Stage Method is designed to protect the writer while providing the very best constructive criticism.

- Stage One: The group makes positive statements only. You are speaking to the writer.

- Stage Two: The writer asks questions about her concerns with the work. This is part of the partnership between writer and critiquer.

- Stage Three: The group makes unsolicited (not based upon writer questions) constructive critical suggestions.

- Civility matters especially in Stage Three when potential "negative" information is delivered.

- The personal response to the writing is unimportant, the emotional depth of response is useful.

- Language is vital. Code words have different meanings so say what you mean, define your response.

- Avoid ist, isms, and other labels.

- "Is it true?" is unimportant and no one's business. Don't ask.

- Use your license as an artist to express yourself with intention.

Feedback on the page

The first step is to read the work. Every new piece of writing a reader approaches is a new adventure regardless of the genre. The reader gets to explore new ideas, new thoughts, new words, and new imagery. When reading for critique purposes, read the work with intention and give the piece at least two if not three good, undistracted reads. The first read is simple: Just read the story the way you would read any other piece of writing. Get the big picture of the work. Have that first experience of meeting the writing on the page (even when that page is a screen). Read the work all the way through completely and if you can, all in one sitting. Go ahead and make a few simple marks on the page if you really must to highlight a significant emotional response or particularly outstanding use of language, but this first read is really all about experiencing the story. Let it whisk you away.

Once you have finished the first read, do a second, more critical read. Now you want to make brief comments on the page. Highlight language, notate issues, circle problems, and add your thoughts about what you are reading and how you experienced it in brief notations along the margins and in the space between the lines. (This is why writers follow the double space, one inch margins convention.) Some writing may require a third read though. Or you may find that by reading the piece out loud, you are able to catch aspects that are missed when you read silently in your head. Once you have completed your critical read through, take some time to sit quietly with the piece and mull it over. Savor the flavor of the words and the emotional experience of the reading or consider the lack of response you may feel because that also is interesting information. After time to digest and consider what you read, move on to written feedback.

There are two parts to your written feedback. First are the line comments in the margins and space between the lines. Make short, concise notations that highlight specific language or an issue or something that particularly struck you, made you laugh, cry or scowl as you read a passage. The second part is the main body of comments which are written on an additional separate page at the end of the piece or on the back of a page of the piece. These comments can be longer than a page; however, one page is a good length. This is where the critique reader elaborates on notated points, uses examples of the work citing language or identifies by page, paragraph or line specific issues or points of the critique. The main body comments are where the critique reader delves into why the different aspects or issues were highlighted in the line comments. The main body is the meat of the critique. In order to be effective and encouraging the critique must be respectful. The following is a four part process for providing critique information that will enable the writer to receive effective and interesting information that will add to the work's continued development.

First, start with positive comments. Every piece of writing contains something good. Find that nugget and extract it. Answer the question: "What did you like about the piece?" Although some writing will challenge the critique reader, look for *something* that worked be that about craft, chronology, character or cause of emotional response. Find the nugget.

"But I really, really didn't like the work!"

So what? You didn't like the work and had this huge emotional reaction called "really, really didn't like the work." Well, then. The writer did an excellent job of effectively creating a significant emotional response in the reader. What caused the response? Develop that chunk of writing ore. (Without the "I didn't like it.")

In the second part, the critique writer asks questions. Where do the questions come from? From those several considered readings of the piece. What questions came up when doing that first and second (or more) read of the work? Was there a place where the reader was knocked out of the reading with the thought "Wait, that doesn't sound right." One very valid question is "I felt (emotion) at this part, is that what you wanted to create?" Questions help the writer by indicating an obstacle for the reader. The questions the critique provider asks clarify or validate what the writer may have attempted to create in the writing. Questions help provide the writer with direction and insight into the effectiveness of her work by providing a glimpse into the reader's experience.

The third part of the written critique requires providing constructive, honest feedback of what did not work well. This is where the critique provider identifies areas that have potential for improvement. This is where the reader stumbled, was removed from the story, or otherwise found difficulty in maintaining the suspension of belief we've all been taught in academic study is integral when reading a good story. Here is where discussion of form or language are appropriate. This is where the meat of craft development is constructed. "I didn't like…" is not appropriate here. What is appropriate is a description of the uncomfortable response, why that response was present (as it relates to the writing), and insight into what might create a different response. The critique provider must remember, that the emotional response is *interesting information* the writer can build upon, discard, or parse as required. Nothing more.

The fourth and concluding part of the written critique

includes a summary of the main issues as the critique provider perceived them and recommended solutions. Cite
what was most positive about the piece. Include any sug-
gested markets if you are aware of them. Remark again
on the best example of language you found in the piece.
Give the writer an overall good point to walk away from
the critique with, a last and final positive thought. And
then sign your name.

Why sign your name? Because a small amount of pride
and ownership goes into putting your name on something.
Attaching your name to your comments implies that you
believe what you are saying and you stand by your own
words. If you sign your name, you are extending a cour-
tesy, and that maintains the paradigm of respecting the
work and the writer and the effort of the critique provider.
Signing your name helps inject civility into the process.

Two helpful recommendations when writing a critique:
No red pen and forego copy editing.

No one wants to be brought back and reminded of high
school or college freshman English class. Use any color
pen you like, just keep in mind that red is a loaded color
for anyone in the United States academic environment.
If that isn't a good enough reason, then just consider that
red is the color of stoplights and stop signs. We want the
writer to write, not stop writing.

Leave the copy editing to the copy editor who comes
later in the process. Just as a first draft is all about getting
the idea onto the page before the writer revises and

corrects errors, so the draft of the work that comes to the group is about the content of the story not the mechanics. Unless a particular grammatical issue really, really bugs you, let it go. The mechanical issues can be caught later in the process, or should be, when the writer puts a piece through copy editing; a step that is integral to polishing a piece before it goes to an agent or publisher or is sent out into the wild world.

Remember—

- Read the work all the way through first, then again for critical thought.

- Some work needs more than two reads.

- Mark up on the pages what stands out or issues you notice during the second read.

- Savor the language.

- Two parts to written feedback: line comments along the page and main body comments at the end.

- Line comments are brief notations or markings of issues or standout lines.

- Main body is more in-depth and specific.

- Main body: Start positive, ask questions (clarify), provide constructive feedback (what didn't work), summarize the main issues then sign your name.

- Liking the work is not important, why is.

- Skip the red pen.

- You are not the copy editor. Editing by committee rarely works out well.

What Do I Critique?

If the process of providing feedback to the writer is not about whether the reader likes the work, then what does the reader critique?

Any issue ever discussed in freshman or high school English when learning about writing or literature is fair game. Look at: plot, consistent verb tense, dialogue, scene, summary, balance of scene and summary, character development, timing, cadence, pace, transitions, technique, point of view, perspective, humor, seriousness, emotional impact, craft, language and more.

If you really don't know where to begin, start with time. What is the chronological thread of the piece? Does too much time elapse while the main character moves from one plot point to another? Does the way time passes make sense? Is it confusing? Does it carry the reader or create obstacles for the reader? Why? Remember, why is a big part of what works or what doesn't work regardless of what aspect you write about.

Passage of time is different than pace. Pace is about the reader's experience of the narrative. Once the narrative grabs the reader's attention, that attention is fed, line by line, paragraph by paragraph, page by page, chapter by chapter. The train chugs up the hill, speeds down in descent, flies over the plain. The reader thrills to the ride, taking in everything that streams by, word after word. How does the pace impact the narrative? Do you feel the tension? Is the story a page turner that can't be put down? Does the story put you to sleep?

Instead of time or pace, look at language. Are there phrases that really stand out? Which lines grab and pull the reader into the piece, stopping time and space? Which lines bring the reader back to reality, breaking the hold of the story? Highlight or underline or circle the lines that really, really strike you as *bold, chilling, hot, fevered, delicous, enticing, inciting...* get the idea?

What about transitions? Were you, the reader, able to keep up with the change of venue, change of point of view, change of perspective, change of character without becoming lost and confused? Did the story make sense as it progressed?

Voice is another critical aspect to explore. Is the voice accurate to the character? Does the ten-year-old female protagonist of a young adult novel have conversations that sound like that of a forty-year-old male? Is the mental image of the character believable? Is the presence of the omniscient narrator effective or distracting? From whose point of view is the story told, character or omniscient narrator? The narrative voice creates the environment as much as any imagery the writer may employ.

If you don't know where to start and chronology, pace, language or transition aren't inviting topics, then answer the simple question "Do I believe the narrator?" Is this a credible narrator? Discuss.

Remember, editors edit. Unless you have a particular pet peeve about a specific grammar issue and the writer keeps hitting that one thing you really, really hate, leave the copyedits to someone else further up the food chain. By the time the writer has the story at the place where mechanical aspects are crucial, it won't be a piece of writing submitted to workshop for copyediting by committee.

Keep in mind what your mother said, watch your language.

A writer has privileged you with the honor of helping her hone her craft. Take that seriously. Be nice. Be truthful. Be honest. Give feedback in a manner in which you would hope it would come to you. Use real words, not labels, or code because those terms (politically correct/incorrect, clichés, trite, culturally descriptive words that end in ist or are isms) mean different things to different people. Instead, define the response you experienced that you want to shorthand by using any of those terms. Any of those code words have *interesting information* at the heart. The critique provider must be willing to do the hard work of dissecting the code word to its essence to explain the reason that it came up. That is the information that can assist the writer. Or not. The writer may look at the slice of information and decide it is not pertinent to the work in progress or is only partially applicable to what is being created.

Look at the work critically, not personally. Finding what you like is usually easy. Defining what you don't like is often the challenge. When you encounter something that didn't work for you, that you didn't like or weren't comfortable with or didn't sound right in your head or feel right in your heart, you have discovered something vitally important. Why was that your response? Furthermore, some of that stuff may actually be the gem, the unearthed ore of the work. Dive into the dark waters of discomfort.

Just as the writer must not take feedback personally, so the critique provider must not be personally attached to her critique. The point of providing feedback is to make an investment in the development of the writer not to showcase your own special skills or highlight how smart you, the reader, is. The critique is not about you, not about the writer, but about the writing. Give honest, accurate, and specific commentary on the work.

After the critique is delivered, let it go.

The simple truth about writers' groups is not everyone in the group will give or know how to give helpful feedback. Some people just want to talk, some people just want to show off and some people will offer hard truths in a courteous, gracious manner and become the people you learn to count on that will help your writing improve. Some comments are worthwhile, some you just disregard.

Your challenge? Be the critique provider that writers want to hear from.

Remember—

- Anything discussed in English class when learning about literature or writing.
- If all else fails, chronological thread, pace or the reader's experience of the narrative, language, transitions, point of view.
- Really don't know where to start: Answer "Do I believe the narrator? Is the narrator credible?"
- Look critically, not personally.
- Don't be attached, your critique is interesting information for the writer, that is all.
- Not everyone can give useful critique. Are you the one writers want to hear from?

About the Author

Victoria A. Hudson lives in Northern California with a family of humans, cats and a dog. She earned a Master of Fine Arts degree in nonfiction writing from Saint Mary's College of California. She was a Founding Fellow at the inaugural Lambda Literary Writers Retreat in 2007. On her blog *Home and Hearth* she writes about food, gardening, pets, and parenting with occasional book reviews and other musings.

Connect with the author online:

Twitter: @vickigeist for literary and life musings or @Vicki_Hudson for updates on her writing and publishing.

Website: http://vickihudson.com/

Blog Home and Hearth:
http://www.throwrockpaperscissors.com/

Facebook:
http://www.facebook.com/VickiHudsonWordsmith

Photo Gallery:
http://vhudson.redbubble.com/

Also available by the Author at Smashwords and other fine e-book venues as a free download: ***Chow***

An Army moves on its stomach but combat rations only go so far, for so long and a Soldier has to find something else to eat. From mess halls to mess kits, Chow *chronicles one Soldier's inventiveness and adventure in food while deployed in wartime. A small snapshot into what many never think about—what's to eat?*

http://www.smashwords.com/books/view/41461

Thanks for reading.

Made in the USA
Charleston, SC
19 January 2013